ATMOSFEAR

written by sean o huigin

illustrated by Barbara Di Lella

BLACK MOSS PRESS
WINDSOR, ONT.

© copyright sean o huigin 1985
Published by Black Moss Press, P.O. Box 143, Station A, Windsor,
Ont. Black Moss Press books are distributed in Canada and the U.S.
by Firefly Books, 3520 Pharmacy Ave., Unit 1-C, Scarborough, Ont.
This book was published with the assistance of the Canada Council
and the Ontario Arts Council.

ISBN 0-88753-134-2

Printed in Canada by Ampersand, Guelph.

this book is dedicated to the future of the world

don't go to
antarctica
don't go near
the ice
there's something
in there lurking
something not so
nice

beneath the drifts
of glittering snow
lies something evil
something low
something with long
icy teeth
something curled up
underneath the
ancient glaciers'
mighty cliffs
with blue cold steely
snarling lips

for centuries
it's lain there
trapped inside
its icy lair
listening as
each year goes
past to the
winter's icy
blast

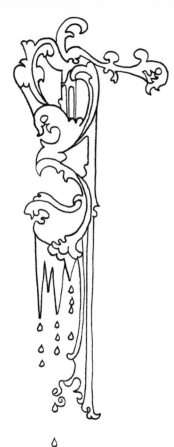

but bit by bit
and drop by drop
as humans make the
air grow hot
pumping garbage
and pollution
they give to it a
neat solution to its
problem of
entrapment
it grinds its jaws
it tries to snap
them

it feels the
ice cap getting
thinner
as the atmosphere
gets grimmer
slowly
daily
drip by drip
it can feel
its prison
slip
turn to water
run away
just a little
every day

but the beast
is old as time
it's in no
rush
it doesn't
whine

someday when the
time has come
we'll hear a
roar
a thunderous drum
come rolling
through our
greying skies
as giant wings
and glaring eyes
rise up from the
earth's south end
we'll see the
icy creature bend
to peer upon our
tiny faces
we will find there
are no places
to escape its
viscious beak
or the claws
upon its feet

take warning now
this is no joke
we're doomed by
all the dust and
smoke we pour into
the air each day
we've got to find
another way

a kinder way to
treat the world
for deep inside
the ice is curled
this bringer of
a nasty fate
and who's to say
it has no mate
a dozen
two
or even five
trapped and waiting
but alive
waiting for we foolish
men to bring about
our own sad end

.

Pollution
Arctic
Dragons
Poetry
1985

DATE DUE